A DRAFT OF L CAVATINAS
(letters to Ez)

A DRAFT OF L CAVATINAS
(letters to Ez)

Brian Strang

Potes & Poets Press
Elmwood CT
2000

Potes & Poets Press *NEW* Chapbook Series #36

for more information about chapbooks in this series,
please write:

Potes & Poets Press
181 Edgemont Avenue
Elmwood CT 06110-1005
http://www.potespoets.org

A DRAFT OF L CAVATINAS
(letters to Ez)

Brian Strang

THE CAVATINAS

cavatina n. [It., dim. of cavata, a separate air] 1. a short, simple solo song or melody that is usually part of a larger composition 2. loosely, an instrumental composition of lyric quality

.

These cavatinas are improvisations on the poetry of Guido Cavalcanti (1250-1300), contemporary and friend of Dante Alighieri and the subject of much study and translation by Ezra Pound. Deliberately unfaithful to the originals, I mistranslated from the Italian, a language of which I have, unfortunately, severely limited knowledge. I also reconfigured the sonnets and ballads into letters, from me to Ez.

In the last year, I have read works about and by Pound and, like many who read him, I am at once in awe of his intellect, humbled by his influence on 20th Century poetics and sometimes alienated by his politics and prejudices. But I'm not trying to praise or bury him; the Ezra of these poems is purely an invention of mine, a subjective and idiosyncratic figure of my own imagining, one made new.

Cavatina I

Go so that you can see past your heart. Svengali keeps track of an
Anglican life (that soprano mistrust of life's love—the daytime land of
great valor). A debunked spirit in the back of a van, a young woman
camping in the park and the show of a wound: these truths of love, distaste
from pressed eggs as eyes. They run between the teeth. If the guns of a
cop dread the first touch, the minds tremble and are at risk—the color of a
soft companion.

Cavatina II

You wanted to get rid of your inspirations—the close cropped hair, the city
golf championship, broad smile, a stockroom full of poisons. You were
cluttered with life when you first set up your little walls—a criminal
record beside the career of an analytical mind. And now you say you have a
divided heart. And when this becomes impossible, you take yourself out of
the bed you made and quit talking and dress yourself as a crucified fairy.
Dusty shelves of skulls and plastic bags, committees reviewing the ability
to charm, poisoned pens and belated greetings. Imagine that you have
conquered yourself up to the ceiling, a pile of bricks so you won't have to
be guarded, cutting little truths in a gigantic mouth.

Cavatina III

And to hell with your valiant flights, for this wristwatch shows more than
right rulings and memory washed perfections. It happened here by
altruistic accident (that I brought from this suspicious egg my
suppression—a strong colored liquid choice). This sobbing is really fucked
up and, no, it is not cut so close to death, accompanying that martyr,
consuming piety in the saloon. Strolling euphoria as naturally blurred
sensations.

Cavatina IV

If I nail this woman to the floor, none will see her nemesis painted
within. You said that song was seasick and vile and might disperse the
purposes of vanity. Where do you go with this new cruelty? Where is the
ripped humility, alert and subtle? You turned toward some fashion of the
times, the animal of porous fangs. None suspected that you had replaced
your heart when such a vicious bath scorches the outside. Now it is time
to pass out some more lies. A figure of a thoughtful person comes to see
and loses at the core.

Cavatina V

Now glean this silly world view—your façade of valor. For who would
dare accuse you while you were in that fiery and paranoid state of mind cut
off from humane contacts? Eventually, in the show of apologies—an era
which you made your servant—you became suspicious and sick and stole
away in dread. In me are the senses removed, in part filled with trembling
people, your cry of classicism. When you lived, all was piety and you said
to me, I know servants who don't give me separate quarters.

Cavatina VI

Plenty for the mind and the anima. The brigands of spirit normally
attached. A less indulgent color—a discontinued eye, puffy and tired.
Look, this grand bravery you wanted to send-"of my dual and convenient
death, by this bella donna, I reenter in vulgar erudition"—doesn't come
collecting with the fury of life. Made of petrified wood or iron or lead,
this door closed on my hand. I would have liked you to have become.

Cavatina VII

Fish swimming through God's eye, that shadow of a sunflower in
kindergarten classrooms. That polarity. Pare away a truth of chasms in
what you see and name. None can carry or count the telling that you read
inch by inch over belated virtues—a gentle beauty you show, your high-
mindedness—a tainted salute we can properly understand.

Cavatina VIII

Death embroiders into your sleeves. Why aren't you furious with me? My
spent eye and your silent witness. Turn down that which you can't call an
approach. It cannot be done in your mind or your integral vision. New
torments arrive crude and actual. Reigning symbols crop away the
inconvenience of someone calling out to you. You have lacerated here,
have come to plane away soft answers losing plenty of thought in the
process, keep your shame guarded closely in your coat.

Cavatina IX

To the senses, come begin to be debased when blind to the active hiccups
of fame, wracked for days with the spasms. This battle of soreness—
manatees brush and quake just below the surface—the old movements of
sponsorship and action, of vortices spinning through the stagnant crowds.
For this, guard against the verses I read—new eyes at your disadvantage if
in flames, if distrusted to the core. And now a need to part from the signs
of the times, of friends in beautiful war, out of necessity or sport.

Cavatina X

You didn't go crawling in protest now that you have been sent for—the
fury of an adorned mind. What pip and volume will you take to the cages
where you will be turned inside out with spotlights and heat? Mountains
turn for you, Taishan, a place you created easily since you believed in
falling. To you comes forward that spirit detailing the disintegrations
through time, truths fleeing. Pressed to the tarmac wire, the cavernous
permanent squint, forms you imagined, bent from the stone, chipping. You
construct and are pooled on the floor. Age cannot send or recover. This
war of shit is dripping from the bars.

Cavatina XI

Possum makes amicable conversation and honeyed desires. In him is no
movement made at the core. Anglican dilettantes racing toward their
favorite cheese shops, condemning in broad strokes while maintaining
elegant snobbery far from muddy American shores. Don't bring that person
within my sight. Some taunt vengeance, you rarefy your requests and build
up such a calamity that animal may really come some day. Within this
disdain is your salute and the sweaty cotton shirt of unrepentant ego. Il
miglior fabbro swings dumb fists in the pottery shop.

Cavatina XII

The business of each is the business of all in this town and something sour
and sweet is lying in the folds of a picnic cloth in the summer weeds.
Inside his coat is a guise, vain lies and poor scraps of paper with
penciled lines ripped vertically from strips of cloth used to preserve a
corpse. A kid convinced of his own genius and, therefore, brilliant in his
derision. Whatever shit is regarded as love, he thinks, with that will I
fill their mouths and be cruel to the men stricken by the fragile lines of
my skull. Death will become tangible and I will become suspicious.

Cavatina XIII

Here lies a subtle spirit, "misunderstood of base minds who comprehend not his power." In mind, the spirit creates disaster. I feel something putrid and vile here in the moon, contrary to the apparitions that tremble begging humility. Move nearer and above you will see in shadow a force of a spirit without mercy.

Cavatina XIV

Certain of intellectual embrace, stamina is granted to those in his wake. Or come up here behind and you will see a crack ready to go through the course of the whole figure. Some shadowy force of personality from the very stone. Shedding skin to remain out of reach. That you are faithful, to see you as you shift. Though you may hear disdain, think only of struggle.

Cavatina XV

Avert your eyes when walking by this monument. Though it may be beautiful, it has been known to drive better people into fits of hysteria. In this world, there is not a single creature who leaves without dying first. And from your single vision, you cannot make company. So what if the man was too difficult to be friends with? Are you ready for the poor and onerous task of lifting up to the silhouette of his face? All sits upon the craft.

Cavatina XVI

Piety comes in many forms, sometimes adorned by the fingers of tragedy. The person of our far reaching lives. What is sensed in the arms of crude return? Certain balance of manic belief and mortality. Providence is our convenience. Find out in the end that this is read as a tale.

Cavatina XVII

Fresh steam rises from the pavement in the brief moment between storms
and the fountains of gutters and drains connect geography, city to country
and land to sea. The sun of that respite and the acute rhyme of feeling and
history, in this unreal city is both comfort and trial. Through a gate as
if a grave, suspect and lit from within, is sent a great plume of smoke
languishing in the eaves. He comes outward from within, unrecognizable.

Cavatina XVIII

At your succinct core, is an armed man, singing of rage and war, an aria
when you appear elaborately, this sea flowing by with bits of silvery
minnows, azure and deep red and small bits of gold. In courage, you
resemble those vile mercenaries of the Vatican. And so much has ascended
to conscience when this land wants you hung from the ceiling. The
similitude of natural ends comes late and comes in red Tuscan soil.

Cavatina XIX

Tired novel and nervous ode! Cat piss and porcupines! So that the
Goodmans of the world will tremble in porous and total Florentine gloss.
The rest is dross. A stinking bird of prey remains on your shoulders. If
your high blood had been discarded, would the vanity have returned you to
your senses? A wonderful sight, rolled in shame. For this putrid animal
splitting your seams, have patience when you run.

Cavatina XX

Confounder of creeping romantics in your battle fettered by vision. All
becomes so many languages and so many places: Navarre, the actual sun,
Ravenna, Aragon, Aquataine and all that representation knows. Come forth
full of validation. Said so to my broken soul: this is no life. For the
eye of your battle, for the rupes in your pockets, your feign of confusion
to save your neck, your eminence, you strut and stutter across my mind.
Whatever seminal invention you choose to forment, call me into the fold
without pity.

Cavatina XXI

While you know I am a scoundrel, you can't deny my sincerity, says he.
Dear mother, please send money. You never fell into this model. Vortices
on your own terms. And your ugliness is truer. That which is not apparent
is that for which you die. In the high guise of the fashion of the times,
I am pressed and left for dada. And some say he is a dead color, living in
a mortal city, among the bricks of words. Return to those streets, this
tragic guide, when life usurps. Ezra drives up in his luminescent
Mercedes. This portion of the story drowns itself in gravity.

Cavatina XXII

In vestments, onerous valour, all thick and good sentiment. Crests and
armory bent toward the basest of marriages. And you had something in
mind when you signed on, though you despised actual movement. The
vegetation just off the runway as you sat for weeks or years in the cage.
Say that you were filled up, that the bars were bulging with special
circumstances, a little tent against the heat and rain, allowance for a short
stack of the best verses. This day over and over. Nothing can be as
tremendous. Contrarian acts of dormancy and return. This guerra di merda
makes you. The sweat of company in your defeat.

Cavatina XXIII

I come here everyday, infuriated that your clarity and good nature have been shed, and find you swimming in vile thoughts. You were careless but elegant in your ability to offend, apart from others, faithful and sharp, rebuking me for my way of life. But now? Through the graves the wind is blowing. I wouldn't give you the time of day since you've turned into such a shit, swaying at the bus stop, pissed off at everyone. That desperation might ease away and let you go.

Cavatina XXIV

If you discover the parts that you have given me along the trails up the hillsides, don't graven my mind away from yours. Write what you must; I am still your servant. Anciently removed. Become fresh, jumping over contact with predecessors. I am under your rain cloud and kicking your junk on the sidewalk.

Cavatina XXV

Look at this wraith that comes up disfigured and brutally divisive. And where will you come to meet us in the future? Are you giving us the runaround? Is this the same one who was so certain, so inquisitive, so decisive? A touch of angina, a torment of will, a malady of suffocation—these treasures of your legacy bind while something deeper apprehends us in our temporary skins. You would die or save yourself by running.

Cavatina XXVI

Certain of your rhymes I chew glassy eyed, an opiate that leadens my heart. In this grave state I apprehend and imagine your death. And you tell me, calling me on a celestial telephone, "Don't send me any more invectives, my mailbox is full." Because this is virtual, I press reply and the splendor of the heavens is jammed electronically. I become weary of the game. And you advance after the storm and creep into my apartment at three in the morning and I hear heavy footfalls in the hallway.

Cavatina XXVII

If you come around here and nobody is home, the semblance of assault, the
place fat and signified, arrangement across the white field. The waves of
superimposed images, lexical spirits and tragedy, a wreck upon your brow.
If, literally, you are that person, if, lately, you are in person in the
form of footsteps, if laments of yore, if tangles of challenge and webs of
deceit and divinations behold... Sruggles and quills and teeth. Be damned
to words and works and nodes.

Cavatina XXVIII

A hard and guarded spiritual song rings placid above a winged vault that is
not one man's to assail. Ez thinks this a stringent place. See verses cut
in the walls of a vale. But please, no piety or pity or suffering for
smooth round surfaces cut in muscular stone. Feeling a sweet hold on
the vortex. Part of the core is sentient.

Cavatina XXIX

Far down in the round hell, a suspicious messenger comes sleeping
through disinvolved company. Brilliant is his attendance of the vision. So
touched and saying was he. In repose, after the creation of all the angels
and devils anyone could need for centuries to come. And I have a special
place for you. If you believe it, hold fast to his young and Norman eyes.
An icon replaces. Loosed from the mooring, signs drift.

Cavatina XXX

The time has now come in our correspondence for some sort of resolution.
The least of these is the most. The challenges are the things themselves.
The surface is the surface. The cat is the dog is the tail. Don't go yet,
we're not done. Planing down a hill obliquely. Suckled end of the
deadening scholar. Disadventure comes of the thrust. The vertebrae click.

Cavatina XXXI

Latent hand racked. Archer shot. Delight in this discomfort-body slumped
and erotic, heroic, napoleonic. Dead member office. Salute as crack is
the third piano. Oh the door swings and well is deep. Well is deep.

Cavatina XXXII

The cage is now forgotten. Perfectly suited for impact, on you established
and now a badge. In the noise, you meddle. In the noise, you call. You
say that you are alive a wire. Matted gray clouds corner you in your
castle. You called to say that you can't say anything. Any shield or
break in your armor. Straight to your glorious ideals, the dichotomy from
one of stuff, of matter that matters most.

Cavatina XXXIII

If you are more gentle in some other imagining, will you lose proportions?
Make this new. Make this over. My face looks upon yours, up at yours. We
are impostors both. Dead in the time of torment, deep in ninth treacherous
flames. "Sweet Death, now is the time you may'st avail me and snatch me
from His hand's hostility." Return now and make me right. Return and
make. The woods are shaggy with new growth and the ground is soft and
wet and black. The treelines are waving. Long and shallow meadows.
Shimmering eyes, wet and black backgrounds.

Cavatina XXXIV

How to part now? Possibilities loom very small. And peace will be
impossible with you. I cut and look out. Imagining you for some kind of
divinity which may turn out to be. You riddle to the core. Guided and
caged.

Cavatina XXXV

A figure is adorned. The face is seen to appear on the side of a glass building at sunset. Crowds gather to witness the miracle. In the end, it might be a face if you look through the eyes of a believer. "Those with crooked eyes see straightway straight." And the face persists and it looks new in this light.

Cavatina XXXVI

Your incurable tragedy and comedy. The sweet fruit makes you puke. You strip the fronts off when you nullify colloquial folly. For that sovereign and much-altered light of love, you are green around the gills.

Cavatina XXXVII

You think that this is being true to your nature and that you are sick and
crazy and it is wonderful to be so. My knees buckle when you say these
things. And my heart is at war with you. So that garrulous pride doesn't
wash away in the stream, make some other excuse and hasten the tempo. It
is easy to have firm opinions in perfect circumstances. Don't show
yourself to be fine tuned when you find yourself deceived. Teeth marks
clear through the middle of my chest. I'll wait for you outside.

Cavatina XXXVIII

The life that is done in and the one that is passing are not among the
noontime celebrations. A similitude of only the loaded and the true.
A perch too low for these games. Intentions are difficult to measure.
A raging move, a toast to "spirit and death." Crude as it may have been,
we vegetate slowly in aftermath.

Cavatina XXXIX

See here your obliteration, not abandoned but occupied in brilliance. You
lie ragged, serving yourself through a gradual heat. And when you sense
you don't believe, why do you look for truth? Some people aren't cut out
for this work. Your static presence figures more stringently in the people
from which you thought yourself removed. A somnambulence. The
sleeper.

Cavatina XL

Banging on the piano, a trope of return and armored cars. The novelty
gives over to a venture of panged species to which you salute. Something
is amiss and agnostic, put to sleep. Disconsolate screaming night and
day. Have your new and modern martini. You have been true, reinvented
and degenerate; you are sick and calling. Lie about on guard against vile-
ness. Lashings to the idea of Ez the abandoned eye. Here is the pain you
sought; your day is second to none.

Cavatina XLI

Forget that you were here once as the eyes of your fair lady. She gives
off a futuristic green light. Taciturn wallowing, unintelligible speech.
Usurp and challenge. Comprehend now that you are a manatee. Born in
your mind is a telepathy and a psychology, thing one and thing two. Your
belladonna, your DaVinci vampyre—contained, tremulous, movements
guarded, salacious. Dive down to the knees. This happy life that you make
of it, this bright and burning cage. More salutes to the expatriates.

Cavatina XLII

In the force of new misadventure, I am dissatisfied to the bone. I am
agitated and porous. Bail me out. Give me a place to go walking. I am
under suspicion and under your name and such adversaries and so much in
this life says to hell with you. In your valor and in your arrogance, in
your comprehensive understanding, in the thick woods, in your wildest
dreams and in your wild oats, in muddled attempts, in botched spite, beside
yourself, right next to you, budding mercy, invectives, torments and
incendiary improprieties. No reckoning, only a long and ugly time made of
discarded ore. Agnostic worth in stillness, in a poverty of ideas, in the
death of grandeur, in the rectangular sun and the tree and knife.

Cavatina XLIII

A new forethought, poor and gentle in love's nuance. I had a small insight
into your chiaroscuro against open light and fields. You gave to all and
agitated at the same time. You with your eyes glassed and filled in your
age. Come and live like a ferret. And with the spirit of a newborn piano,
in the middle of unctuous guilt, all my life was obscured and distressed.
You said this and then broke up laughing and said, "Guard, come get these
Philistines from outta my face." Cut to ribbons of repose at your side.
In your rancor and suffering, the high and mercenary figure collapses. The
treatment and lassitude and splendor that cannot be seen but with rigor.
So back to this tough question and porous argument. I asked you to
remember Toulouse and the affair you had there. Send for the things
you'll need and if she is there to receive you, she'll come as far as the
river. Quick and strong and in your raging cups, you cut out your own
eyes. Go back and you will find the remains of this story.

Cavatina XLIV

Sly wink, hands waving or saluting, call it what you will or don't call it
anything. She is my fire and holds for me what I hold for her in my heart.
This is no ordinary spirit of love. But I sit here full of suspicion and
irony. What ragged lies do I cling to? Am I a martyr to anything? It
pains me to think how jaded and aloof I have become. In the guise of the
dance, throw away dissatisfactions that keep you at a safe distance.
This wounded world converges and diverges, guaranteed of ending and of
beginning and so on. Anguish keeps you from acceptance, courtesy keeps you
waiting.

Cavatina XLV

In a dark wood. Isn't that how it begins, these trials and tribulations?
The stars above give perspective. At the bonded and recalcitrant chapel in
a rose-colored window, the scales on the walls belie the fossilized
intimacy and ornamentation. Salutes go immediately to the country, the
repose of only what you find. This is a hard lesson. Why didn't you tell
me of your condition? Had I known, I would have brought you something.
This stagnant pastoral has lifted the sun and an embrace has
withered—lovingly transcendent. A fresh and leafy place under the tree.
My words cannot be true.

Cavatina XLVI

I can see something new and dire on the horizon for you. What you find
dear will be for sale. Your new sensation of composition will become as
common as gentle avenues leading to the center of the city. And you will
be revered and hated and cursed and saluted. It is your bilious conscience
that makes this so. A wicked fate, a twisted wreck saving money in an
asylum, your intellectual vision. You want mercy and mercy you must
give. You become even more new. I make myself older. Dig deeper into
your pious verses as they are you.

Cavatina XLVII

Perched on the hill above Tuscany, with legs like pianos dripping with the melodious, you are molten and onerous. Your new door into the people around you is inimitable. And I am certain that you will contest the truth of this even after death-new pains make you stringent and abandoned. In the heart of this matter a tumultuous thunder sounds. Amorous nature gives way to your orders. Breathe deeper to your servants. Part the way through the crowd. Sweet intellect, sharp knife, startled place, adore.

Cavatina XLVIII

A rite of purification, the working of hallowed sights almost without mercy. A soaking to refined conquests. The nice and clean cantos, the ones of certitude die in the salted ground. And born from inside, formed of a new persona with carnivorous aim, what guides is felt. I believe that you came along this path through the death of reason but you came unwillingly by mischance. A great penchant for tragedy, you arrived and asked for gratitude.

Cavatina XLIX

Only piety has been lost so you ended up. Digest this and thank yourself
for the battle. Somehow you didn't become disenchanted; even bitterness
and collapse became luminous. Duress was hard-won and you became
wrought . How you hated life then. And you showed through your seams.
Cover your eyes with scales.

Cavatina L

At last irksome vanity and pain are set aside. They fall as I condemn—my
projected shadow. Wounds I suffer myself in spirit. Hold away the flame.